HORSE RAID

ODYSSEY

For my two boys, Connor and Jack — S.K.

For my wife, Deborah and my daughters, Allison and Caitlin — B.F.

Illustrations copyright © 1998 Bill Farnsworth.
Book copyright © 1998 Trudy Corporation, 353 Main Avenue, Norwalk, CT 06851,
and the Smithsonian Institution, Washington, DC, 20560.

Soundprints is a division of Trudy Corporation, Norwalk, Connecticut.

Book layout: Diane Hinze Kanzler

First Edition 1998
10 9 8 7 6 5 4 3 2 1
Printed in Hong Kong

Acknowledgments:
   Our thanks to Jane Walsh and JoAllyn Archambault of the Department of Anthropology at the Smithsonian Institution's National Museum of Natural History for their curatorial review.

Library of Congress Cataloging-in-Publication Data

Korman, Susan
    Horse Raid : An Arapaho Camp in the 1800s / by Susan Korman ; illustrated by Bill Farnsworth.
        p.   cm. — (Odyssey)
    Summary: While visiting the Smithsonian Institution's Museum of Natural History to see the Native Cultures of the Americas exhibit, Kevin travels back in time to an Arapaho Indian camp in the mid-1800s.
        ISBN 1-56899-613-6 (hardcover)   ISBN 1-56899-614-4 (pbk.)
        1. Arapaho Indians — Juvenile Fiction.   [1. Arapaho Indians — Fiction.
    2. Time travel — Fiction.]   I. Farnsworth, Bill, ill.   II. Title.   III. Series: Odyssey (Smithsonian Institution)
    PZ7.K83693Ho   1998   98-6008
    [E] — dc21   CIP
                                                                                                   AC

HORSE RAID

Written by Susan Korman
Illustrated by Bill Farnsworth

Soundprints
Where Children Discover…

"Where have you been, Kevin?" Tomas asks. "You were supposed to meet us twenty minutes ago." Lucy, Emma, and Tomas have been waiting for Kevin at the entrance to the Native Cultures of the Americas exhibit in the Smithsonian Institution's Museum of Natural History.

"Sorry, guys," says Kevin as he hurries up. "My dad took me to a tryout for the traveling soccer team."

"I didn't know you were going out for the traveling team!" Lucy says. "That's great!"

"I guess..." Kevin says, but he's not so sure. He changes the subject. "Let's check out the Plains Indians exhibit first, okay?"

As they round the corner into the exhibit, the first thing they see is a tall tipi.

"Wow," breathes Emma. "That is so cool!"

Kevin wanders over to the other side of the display. A sign on the wall says the tipi was the home of an Arapaho family before 1875.

"The tipi cover was stitched together from fourteen buffalo hides," Lucy reads aloud.

Kevin gazes at the lifelike figures of the Arapahos inside the tipi. He wonders what life was like for the Indians.

The museum walls fade. The next thing Kevin knows, he's standing in a grassy field, dressed in a buckskin shirt, leggings, and moccasins. Nearby, dozens of Arapaho women are pitching tipis.

I'm at a real Arapaho camp! Kevin realizes.

The women have set long poles in the ground. Kevin watches as the women stretch the covers over the frames and fasten them to the ground with pegs.

"Yellow Bear!"

Kevin sees that a woman is beckoning to him. "Come, Yellow Bear," she calls.

As he follows her into a tipi, Kevin notices the inside is lined with a decorated curtain made of panels tied to the tipi frame. It is edged in colorful painted designs with drawings of men hunting buffalo and riding horses.

The woman piles sticks and dung chips in the center of the dirt floor under the smoke-hole at the top of the tipi. Then she begins to light a fire. "Yellow Bear," she says while she works, "your father and uncles will soon return from the buffalo hunt. They will need your help."

Before Kevin can reply, excited shouts can be heard outside. The hunters have returned!

Outside, Kevin helps the men unload the buffalo meat and skins. The women begin preparing the meat and hides for drying. As the men work, they laugh and shout—a sign that the hunt was successful.

As Kevin helps his Arapaho father, Little Hawk, he sees a gray-haired man gesturing angrily at a younger man.

"What is happening?" Kevin asks.

"My brother, Sitting Eagle, is angry with Wolf Moccasin," Little Hawk explains. "It was your cousin's first hunt and their family's hunting horse was killed by a buffalo."

Kevin remembers reading that Indian males tried to win honor through their bravery on the dangerous buffalo hunts. Instead, Wolf Moccasin has brought hardship to his family. Without a trained hunting horse, it will be difficult for them in the hunt. Kevin feels bad for his Arapaho cousin.

Later, there is a big feast to celebrate the successful hunt. All night long, families visit Kevin's tipi. His mother, whose name is Eagle Woman, boils buffalo meat and turnips over the fire.

Kevin's father, Little Hawk, is the host and sits opposite the doorway. Kevin and the rest of the males sit on his left. The women and Kevin's younger sister, Red Paint Girl, sit on Little Hawk's right.

The men laugh and tell stories about the hunt. Kevin listens
as they talk about their swift horses and their own skill as hunters.
At last it is time to go to bed. Kevin crawls onto
his bed of trade blankets and buffalo robes. It is soft
and warm and Kevin is soon asleep.

14

In the morning the women hang the fresh buffalo meat from a high rail held up by poles to dry in the sun and wind. The poles are tall, so that hungry dogs cannot steal the meat. The women work hard scraping flesh and hair from buffalo hides. Then they stretch the hides out on the ground to dry.

In the afternoon, Kevin joins some younger boys playing a game with a hoop and pole.

"What are you doing playing children's games, Yellow Bear?" says an older boy. "You will soon be old enough to join our Kit Fox lodge."

Kevin knows the boy is talking about the first society Arapaho boys join, where they learn how to hunt and become men.

"Two Crows!" another boy shouts as he runs up. "They are planning to raid a Comanche camp. My uncle says that some of us can go along!"

A horse raid! Kevin feels a tingle of excitement. He has read about the daring theft of horses from the camps of other tribes. "May I go?" he asks.

"Perhaps, but first you must consult Goes-In-Lodge," the boy named Two Crows replies. "Today the war leader is on a vision quest. He is alone in the hills, fasting and calling on spirit powers for the raid. He will be back at sundown. You can ask him then."

Later that night, Kevin finds Goes-In-Lodge in his tipi. The war leader is drinking mint tea by the fire. "Come in, Yellow Bear," he says.

Taking a deep breath, Kevin tells Goes-In-Lodge why he has come.

For several minutes, the war leader stares down into a wooden bowl filled with buffalo blood. "I see a vision, Yellow Bear," he tells Kevin. "I see a strong horse. It is a sign that you are ready to go on the raid."

Kevin's stomach tightens. He thinks of what happened to Wolf Moccasin during the buffalo hunt. *What if I can't prove my bravery during the horse raid?* Kevin wonders.

"You will need this." The war leader holds out a knife in a decorated leather sheath.

Kevin takes the knife from Goes-In-Lodge. As he ties the thongs of the sheath around his waist, he vows to do his best.

The next day, Kevin joins the others as they paint their faces. The horses are painted, too. Kevin learns that this is done to attract the help of spirits during the dangerous raid.

When the band of raiders is ready, Kevin rides alongside his father. They head east, where a Comanche camp has been sighted.

They ride for a long time. The sun beats down as they cross grassy plains. The hot, dry breeze provides little relief. By mid-afternoon Kevin's legs and back feel sore and tired.

At last the group stops near a river. Two of the men disguise themselves in wolf skins. Kevin is puzzled, until Little Hawk explains they are scouts who will sneak ahead to see if there are horses at the Comanche camp.

The scouts return with good news. They have spotted dozens of horses! The men plan the raid for tomorrow at dawn.

It is still dark when the Arapahos line up along a ridge overlooking the Comanche village. Streaks of pink already show in the east where the sun is rising. Kevin knows they must make their move quickly, before daybreak.

The raiders steal down the hill and into the quiet Comanche camp. A few men quickly cut the hobbles from some horses and ride away with them. Two Crows points out a sturdy-looking packhorse, but Kevin has spotted another—a lean and handsome stallion. The leather rope around its neck runs across the ground and disappears beneath the edge of a tipi.

"That's the Comanche chief's horse!" Two Crows whispers. "Only the bravest, most experienced raiders dare to take a horse that is tied to its owner!"

Kevin knows he should listen to Two Crows, but he cannot take his eyes off the handsome stallion. Sliding off his own horse, he steps closer, glad that his moccasins make no sound. The horse whickers and Kevin freezes. Luckily, no Comanche stirs. Drawing the sharp knife from its sheath, he cuts the stallion's tether and hobble. In one smooth motion, he is on the horse's back and riding away. His own horse races after them.

An outraged shout splits the quiet morning. A Comanche has spotted the raiders!

As more Comanches rush outside, Little Hawk and other men raise their bows and fire arrows.

Kevin bends low over the stallion's neck, urging him on. Arrows and spears fly all around him. One narrowly misses his ear. Kevin's heart pounds in his chest as the stallion speeds toward the hills, carrying him to safety.

By late morning, the last of the raiders has arrived at the meeting spot in the hills. Kevin is relieved that no one has been injured. Everyone is amazed at his handsome prize and his brave theft from a Comanche chief!

Cheers greet the raiders as they ride into camp with the new horses. Two Crows tells everyone the story of Kevin's bravery. As Kevin dismounts, several boys rush over to him.

"Come, Yellow Bear," they say. "We are getting ready for the Kit Fox ceremony. It is time for you to join us."

Kevin learns special traditional songs and dances that the lodge will perform in their ceremony for the rest of the camp.

The lodge adviser tells Kevin that at the ceremony he must present a gift to an older member of their lodge. Kevin thinks hard about what to choose for his offering. Then an idea comes to him.

The next day, Kevin and the others fast all day long. Their faces are painted, and they dress in brightly-colored ceremonial clothing. As a sign of his exceptional bravery, Kevin is given a lance to carry. The drums beat slowly as the Kit Fox members begin their dance in the center of the camp circle. Kevin chants and dances with his lodge.

The time comes for Kevin to present his gifts. He gives a deer-skin quiver to the Kit Fox adviser and a metal bracelet to Two Crows, as thanks for helping him go on the raid. Then he nods to his father, Little Hawk.

Little Hawk brings forward Kevin's prized possession—the Comanche chief's stallion. Kevin takes the horse's bridle and leads it over to his cousin, Wolf Moccasin.

"This is a gift for you," he says to his cousin.

Wolf Moccasin stands as straight as an arrow. Kevin cannot read the look in his eyes. Has he made a mistake with his choice of gifts?

Finally, Wolf Moccasin speaks. "Your generosity honors you, Yellow Bear. I am pleased to have such a horse for hunting."

Across the circle, Little Hawk's eyes shine. The gift of a horse, so valuable to the buffalo hunters, is a great act of generosity and will earn Kevin the respect of everyone there.

Drumbeats fill the air. His heart full, Kevin returns to the circle of dancers.

29

As Kevin's feet pound out the beat, he looks down. He is no longer wearing moccasins and buckskin, but plain old sneakers and jeans. He is back in the museum.

Lucy peers at him closely. "Are you okay? You're acting kind of weird today."

Kevin finds himself talking about what was bothering him earlier. "My dad wants me to join the traveling soccer team, and I'm not sure I want to do it," he tells them.

"Why don't you just tell your dad the truth?" Lucy suggests.

"My dad's the coach. I don't want to disappoint him. I don't want him to think I'm scared..." Kevin's voice trails off.

Tomas shrugs. "Well, if you're not scared, what's the big deal?"

They move on to a display of beadwork and quillwork. Kevin's eyes lock on a pair of moccasins. They remind him of the pair he was just wearing.

I was brave then, he thinks. *I can be brave now, too*!

"You know? You guys are right," he says. "When I get home, I'm going to tell my dad I want to do it."

"All *right*!" his friends cheer as they head for the next exhibit.

About the Plains Indians

Less than two hundred years ago, Native American tribes were living in the Great Plains of what is now the central United States. A number of these tribes were nomadic, moving from place to place at different times of the year. They included the Assiniboine, Blackfoot, Cheyenne, Comanche, Crow, Kiowa, Lakota, and Arapaho.

Nomadic tribes hunted deer, moose, and elk, but their lives centered around the buffalo. Buffalo meat provided food; their hides provided shelter and clothing; the buffalo horn, bone, and leather were used for tools and ornaments. Buffalo chips—dried buffalo dung—were used as a fuel for fires, since there were few trees on the plains.

In the winter, each tribe stayed in a favorite camp where there was wood, water, and shelter from the wind, but in warmer months they all followed the herds of buffalo.

Nomadic tribes needed good horses to hunt buffalo, and they needed pack horses to carry their belongings from place to place. Tribes would guard their horses closely, and horse raids were common.

Nomadic tribes lived in tipis—tents made of buffalo hides that were cut and sewn together, then stretched over long poles and fastened with peeled sticks called pins. Women made and cared for the tipis and could put them up and take them down in just a few minutes. Tipis could be rolled up and tied to a travois—a kind of sled that was pulled by a horse. The travois had a platform between two long poles, and was used to haul supplies and even people from one camp to the next.

Six-foot-high liners were hung inside the tipis. The airspace between the tipi and the liner created insulation and a current of air that pulled the smoke from the fire up and out of the smoke-hole at the top. Some families painted their liners with colorful designs or pictures of warriors. Liners also gave the family privacy. Without liners, their shadows, cast by the fire, could be seen from the outside. Each family member had a certain place in the tipi to sleep and keep personal belongings.

Some tribes had societies called "lodges." They were clubs that met for religious, social, or military purposes. The first of six lodges an Arapaho male would join over his lifetime was the Kit Fox lodge. In this lodge teenage boys learned to support and help each other while they learned hunting and raiding skills. For respected Arapaho women, there was the Sacred Buffalo lodge. One of the most basic Arapaho values was generosity. An unselfish person who gave to the needy was praised and highly respected.

Plains Indians also had religious ceremonies to honor the spirits of the natural world. Most men and some women went on vision quests, where they would go off alone, away from the camp, to fast and pray.

Modern Plains Indians still live in the Great Plains and some tribes have their own buffalo herds. Some Indians live on reservations. Others live in urban areas along with Americans from all backgrounds. Modern Plains Indians dress, attend school, and live like other Americans in the United States. While modern Plains Indians no longer hunt buffalo for survival, they continue to practice and honor the customs of their ancestors.

Glossary

band: A group of people bound together by family ties and a need to share in work or self-defense.

beadwork: Small glass beads gotten from traders that are sewn or woven into patterns by Native American women and used to decorate weapons, clothing, tools, and other household objects.

buckskin: Deerskin; a soft leather often used for clothing.

hobble: A leather rope or thongs that tie a horse's legs so it can take only small steps. A hobble prevents the horse from running away.

vision quest: A retreat made by Native Americans. They fast—eat little or nothing and drink only tea and/or water—and go off alone to pray, hoping for a sign, guidance, or help from the spirits they believe live in all things in nature.